Walden

Mountain maple leaves.

When I wrote the following pages, or rather the bulk of them, I lived alone, in the woods, a mile from any neighbor, in a house which I had built myself, on the shore of Walden Pond, in Concord, Massachusetts. I lived there two years and two months. At present I am a sojourner in civilized life again.

Henry D. Thoreau.

Again I scent the white water-lily, and a season I had waited for is arrived.... It is the emblem of purity, and its scent suggests it. Growing in stagnant and muddy [water], it bursts up so pure and fair to the eye and so sweet to the scent, as if to show us what purity and sweetness reside in ... the slime and muck of the earth.

Journal, June 16, 1854

Water lilies and pads.

Thoreau's
WALDEN

Selections from his Masterpiece
and his **Journal**

By the Editors
of Country Beautiful

Photography
by Dorothy May Small

COUNTRY BEAUTIFUL
CORPORATION
24198 WEST BLUEMOUND ROAD
WAUKESHA, WISCONSIN 53186

Selections from *Walden* are unmarked;
Journal selections are dated.

COUNTRY BEAUTIFUL: *Publisher and Editorial Director:* Michael P. Dineen; *Vice President, Editorial:* Robert L. Polley; *Vice President, Operations:* Donna Griesemer; *Managing Editor:* John M. Nuhn (House Editor); *Art Director:* Buford Nixon; *Senior Editors:* James H. Robb, Kenneth L. Schmitz, Stewart L. Udall; *Associate Editors:* Wendy Weirauch, Joseph John; *Editorial Assistant:* Julie Fischer; *Art Assistant:* Ann Baer; *Production:* John Dineen; *Assistant to Publisher:* Gay Ciesinski; *Administration:* Rita Brock, Karen Ladewig, Dolores Wangert, Janet Forbes, Chris Maynard; *Distribution Center:* James Haraughty.

Country Beautiful Corporation is a wholly owned subsidiary of the Flick-Reedy Corporation: President: Frank Flick; Secretary-Treasurer: R. L. Robertson; Assistant Secretary-Treasurer: August Caamano.

Library of Congress Cataloging in Publication Data

Thoreau, Henry David, 1817-1862.
  Thoreau's Walden.

  I. Thoreau, Henry David, 1817-1862. Journal. Selections. 1976. II. Title. III. Title: Walden.
PS3048.A35 1976   818'.3'09   76-27358
ISBN 0-87294-110-8

Frosted twigs and branches.

So sweet and wholesome is the winter, so simple and moderate, so satisfactory and perfect, that her children will never weary of it. What a poem! an epic in blank verse, enriched with a million tinkling rhymes. It is solid beauty.

Journal, December 7, 1856

Nature never makes haste; her systems revolve at an even pace. The bud swells imperceptibly, without hurry or confusion, as though the short spring days were an eternity.

Journal, September 17, 1839

Pink peony bloom and bud.

Confronting
Life Deliberately

I went to the woods to live deliberately,
to front only the essential facts of life, and see
if I could not learn what it had to teach, and not,
when I came to die, discover that I had not lived.
I did not wish to live what was not life. . . . nor
did I wish to practice resignation, unless
it was quite necessary.

*It was a pleasant hillside where
I worked, covered with pine woods,
and a small open field where pines
and hickories were springing up...*

ear the end of March, 1845, I borrowed an axe and
went down to the woods by Walden Pond, nearest to where
I intended to build my house, and began to cut down some
tall arrowy white pines, still in their youth, for timber. . . .
It was a pleasant hillside where I worked, covered with
pine woods, through which I looked out on the pond, and a
small open field in the woods where pines and hickories
were springing up.

Spruce and pine trees.

Snow geese at sunset.

*The geese rose up with a great flapping
of wings at the signal of their commander,
circled over my head and steered to Canada . . .*

I was startled by the *honking* of geese flying low over the woods, like weary travelers getting in late from southern lakes, and indulging at last in unrestrained complaint and mutual consolation. Standing at my door, I could hear the rush of their wings; when, driving toward my house, they suddenly spied my light, and with hushed clamor wheeled and settled in the pond. So I came in, and shut the door, and passed my first spring night in the woods.

In the morning I watched the geese from the door through the mist, sailing in the middle of the pond, fifty rods off, so large and tumultuous that Walden appeared like an artificial pond for their amusement. But when I stood on the shore they at once rose up with a great flapping of wings at the signal of their commander, and when they had got into rank circled about over my head, twenty-nine of them, and then steered straight to Canada, with a regular *honk* from the leader at intervals, trusting to break their fast in muddier pools. A "plump" of ducks rose at the same time and took the route to the north in the wake of their noisier cousins.

Perhaps on the spring morning when Adam and Eve were driven out of Eden Walden Pond was already in existence, and even then breaking up in a gentle spring rain accompanied with mist and a southerly wind, and covered with myriads of ducks and geese, which had not heard of the fall, when still such pure lakes sufficed them. Even then it had commenced to rise and fall, and had clarified its waters and colored them of the hue they now wear, and obtained a patent of Heaven to be the only Walden Pond in the world and distiller of celestial dews. Who knows in how many unremembered nations' literatures this has been the Castalian Fountain? or what nymphs presided over it in the Golden Age? It is a gem of the first water which Concord wears in her coronet.

I have penetrated to those meadows on the morning of many a first spring day, jumping from hummock to hummock, from willow root to willow root, when the wild river valley and the woods were bathed in so pure and bright a light as would have waked the dead, if they had been slumbering in their graves, as some suppose. There needs no stronger proof of immortality. All things must live in such a light.

Perhaps on the morning when Adam and
Eve were driven out Walden Pond was already
in existence, even then breaking up in a rain
and covered with myriads of ducks and geese . . .

Oak tree and lichen-covered rocks.

The earth is not a mere fragment of
dead history, stratum upon stratum like
the leaves of a book, but living
poetry like the leaves of a tree ...

The earth is not a mere fragment of dead history, stratum upon stratum like the leaves of a book, to be studied by geologists and antiquaries chiefly, but living poetry like the leaves of a tree, which precede flowers and fruit — not a fossil earth, but a living earth; compared with whose great central life all animal and vegetable life is merely parasitic.

The habit of looking at things microscopically, as the lichens on the trees and rocks, really prevents my seeing aught else in a walk. Would it not be noble to study the shield of the sun on the thallus of the sky, cerulean, which scatters its infinite sporules of light through the universe? To the lichenist is not the shield (or rather the apothecium) of a lichen disproportionately large compared with the universe?

Journal, March 5, 1852

Love is the burden of all Nature's odes;
the marriage of the flowers spots the meadows and
fringes the hedges with pearls and diamonds . . .

Love is the burden of all Nature's odes. The song of the birds is an epithalamium, a hymeneal. The marriage of the flowers spots the meadows and fringes the hedges with pearls and diamonds. In the deep water, in the high air, in woods and pastures, and the bowels of the earth, this is the employment and condition of all things.

Journal, March 2, 1840

In love we impart, each to each, in subtlest immaterial form of thought or atmosphere, the best of ourselves, such as commonly vanishes or evaporates in aspirations, and mutually enrich each other. The lover alone perceives and dwells in a certain human fragrance. To him humanity is not only a flower, but an aroma and a flavor also.

Journal, September 23, 1852

Pink trillium bloom.

Mule deer fawn.

It is remarkable how many creatures
live wild and free though secret in the
woods, and still sustain themselves
in the neighborhood of towns . . .

It is remarkable how many creatures live wild and free though secret in the woods, and still sustain themselves in the neighborhood of towns, suspected by hunters only.

Summer begins now, about a week past, with the expanded leaves, the shade, and warm weather. Cultivated fields, too, are leaving out, that is, corn and potatoes coming up. Most trees are leaved and are now forming fruit. Young berries, too, are forming, and birds are being hatched. . . . It is now the season of growth. Have not wild animals now henceforth their young, and fishes, too?

Journal, June 1, 1853

The air is now pretty full of shad flies, and there is an incessant sound made by the fishes leaping for such as are struggling on the surface. It sounds like the lapsing of a swift stream sucking amid rocks. The fishes make a business of thus getting their evening meal, dimpling the river like large drops, as far as I can see, sometimes making a loud plashing. Meanwhile, the kingfishers are on the look-out for the fishes as they rise, and I saw one dive in the twilight and go off uttering his cr-r-rack-cr-r-rack.

Journal, June 9, 1854

The night-hawk circled overhead in
the sunny afternoon like a mote in the eye,
falling from time to time with a swoop . . .

The night-hawk circled overhead in the sunny afternoon—for I sometimes made a day of it—like a mote in the eye, or in heaven's eye, falling from time to time with a swoop and a sound as if the heavens were rent, torn at last to very rags and tatters, and yet a seamless cope remained; small imps that fill the air and lay their eggs on the ground on bare sand or rocks on the tops of hills, where few have found them; graceful and slender like ripples caught up from the pond, as leaves are raised by the wind to float in the heavens; such kindredship is in Nature. The hawk is aerial brother of the wave which he sails over and surveys, those his perfect air-inflated wings answering to the elemental unfledged pinions of the sea. Or sometimes I watched a pair of hen-hawks circling high in the sky, alternately soaring and descending, approaching and leaving one another, as if they were the embodiment of my own thoughts. Or I was attracted by the passage of wild pigeons from this wood to that, with a slight quivering winnowing sound and carrier haste; or from under a rotten stump my hoe turned up a sluggish, portentous, and outlandish spotted salamander, a trace of Egypt and the Nile, yet our contemporary. When I paused to lean on my hoe, these sounds and sights I heard and saw anywhere in the row, a part of the inexhaustible entertainment which the country offers.

Blue flag iris.

The blue flag iris grows thinly in the
pure water, rising from the stony bottom . . .

This pond has rarely been profaned by a boat, for there is little in it to tempt a fisherman. Instead of the white lily, which requires mud, or the common sweet flag, the blue flag (*Iris versicolor*) grows thinly in the pure water, rising from the stony bottom all around the shore, where it is visited by hummingbirds in June; and the color both of its bluish blades and its flowers and especially their reflections, are in singular harmony with the glaucous water.

Still grows the vivacious lilac a generation after the door and lintel and the sill are gone, unfolding its sweet-scented flowers each spring, to be plucked by the amusing traveler; planted and tended once by children's hands, in front yard plots—now standing by wall-sides in retired pastures, and giving place to new-rising forests—the last of that strip, sole survivor of that family. Little did the dusky children think that the puny slip with its two eyes only, which they stuck in the ground in the shadow of the house and daily watered, would root itself so, and outlive them, and house itself in the rear that shaded it, and grown man's garden and orchard, and tell their story faintly to the lone wanderer a half century after they had grown up and died — blossoming as fair, and smelling as sweet, as in that first spring. I mark its still tender, civil, cheerful, lilac colors.

*In a pleasant spring day all
men's sins are forgiven; such a
day is a truce to vice . . .*

A single gentle rain makes the grass many shades greener. So our prospects brighten on the influx of better thoughts. We should be blessed if we lived in the present always, and took advantage of every accident that befell us, like the grass which confesses the influence of the slightest dew that falls on it; and did not spend our time in atoning for the neglect of past opportunities, which we call doing our duty. We loiter in winter while it is already spring. In a pleasant spring morning all men's sins are forgiven. Such a day is a truce to vice.

Near at hand, upon the topmost spray of a birch, sings the brown-thrasher—or red mavis, as some love to call him—all the morning, glad of your society, that would find out another farmer's field if yours were not here. While you are planting the seed, he cries, "Drop it, drop it—cover it up, cover it up—pull it up, pull it up, pull it up." But this was not corn, and so it was safe from such enemies as he.

A phoebe soon built in my shed, and a robin for protection in a pine which grew against the house. In June the partridge (*Tetrao umbellus*), which is so shy a bird, led her brood past my windows, from the woods in the rear to the front of my house, clucking and calling to them like a hen, and in all her behavior proving herself the hen of the woods. The young suddenly disperse on your approach, at a signal from the mother, as if a whirlwind had swept them away, and they so exactly resemble the dried leaves and twigs that many a traveler has placed his foot in the midst of a brood, and heard the whir of the old bird as she flew off, and her anxious calls and mewing, or seen her trail her wings to attract his attention, without suspecting their neighborhood.

I see a white spider with two reddish spots;
I saw the other day a spider on a primrose . . .

Lysimachia stricta, upright loosetrife, now well out, by
Hosmer's Pond and elsewhere, a rather handsome flower or
cylindrical raceme of flowers. The *Castanea vesca* [chestnut]
with cream-colored flowers, seen from far, and the small green
burs just forming. This is before the bass, methinks. It is
covered with insects, now that tree flowers are scarce — rose-
bugs, a kind of locust, and I see a milk-white spider with two
reddish spots; — a rather disagreeable buttery scent. I saw the
other day a spider on a dwarf primrose, yellow, like the flower,
and shaped like a flower.

Journal, July 6, 1852

I saw a cherry-bird peck from the middle of its upright
(vertical) web on a rush of one of those large (I think yellow-
marked) spiders within a rod of me. It dropped to the ground,
and then the bird picked it up. It left a hole or rent in the middle
of the web. The spider cunningly spreads his net for feebler
insects, and then takes up his post in the center, but perchance
a passing bird picks him from his conspicuous station.

Journal, August 26, 1859

Crab spider on lady's slipper bloom.

For Want of
a Little Common Sense

My purpose in going to Walden Pond was
not to live cheaply nor to live dearly there, but
to transact some private business with the fewest
obstacles; to be hindered from accomplishing
which for want of a little common sense, a
little enterprise and business talent, appeared
not so sad as foolish.

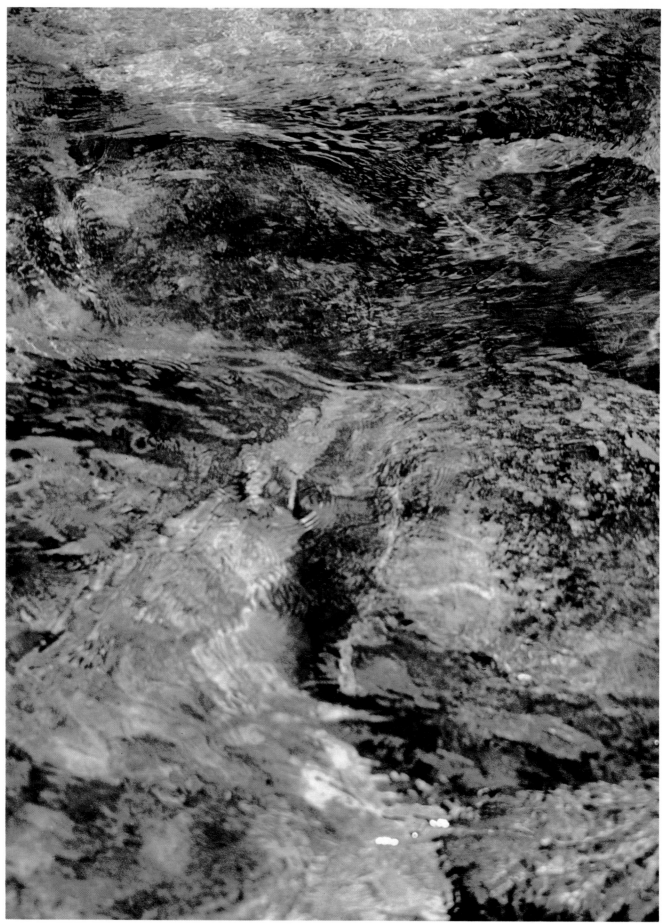

Shallow stream.

*A field of water continually
receives new life and motion from above . . .*

A field of water betrays the spirit that is in the air. It is continually receiving new life and motion from above. It is intermediate in its nature between land and sky. On land only the grass and trees wave, but the water itself is rippled by the wind. I see where the breeze dashes across it by the streaks or flakes of light. It is remarkable that we can look down on its surface.

All our Concord waters have two colors at least; one when viewed at a distance, and another, more proper, close at hand. The first depends more on the light, and follows the sky. In clear weather, in summer, they appear blue at a little distance, especially if agitated, and at a great distance all appear alike. In stormy weather they are sometimes of a dark slate color. . . . Walden is blue at one time and green at another, even from the same point of view. Lying between the earth and the heavens, it partakes of the color of both. Viewed from a hilltop it reflects the color of the sky; but near at hand it is of a yellowish tint next the shore where you can see the sand, then a light green, which gradually deepens to a uniform dark green in the body of the pond.

What more luxuriant than a clover field;
this is the most characteristic feature of June . . .

What more luxuriant than a clover field. The poorest soil that is covered with it looks incomparably fertile. This is perhaps the most characteristic feature of June, resounding with the hum of insects, such a blush on the fields. The rude health of the sorrel cheek has given place to the blush of clover. Painters are wont, in their pictures of Paradise, to strew the field too thickly with flowers. There should be moderation in all things. Though we love flowers we do not want them so thick under our feet that we cannot walk without treading on them. But a clover field in bloom is some excuse for them.

Journal, June 15, 1853

It commonly chances that I make my most interesting botanical discoveries when I [am] in a thrilled and expectant mood, perhaps wading in some remote swamp where I have just found something novel and feel more than usually remote from town. Or some rare plant which for some reason has occupied a strangely prominent place in my thoughts for some time will present itself. My expectation ripens to discovery. I am prepared for strange things.

Journal, September 2, 1856

Dew on clover blossom.

Bullmoose.

How much more conversant was the Indian with any wild animal or plant than we are; how many words in his language about a moose or birch bark . . .

How much more conversant was the Indian with any wild animal or plant than we are, and in his language is implied all that intimacy, as much as ours is expressed in our language. How many words in his language about a moose, or birch bark, and the like! The Indian stood nearer to wild nature than we.... It was a new light when my guide gave me Indian names for things for which I had only scientific ones before. In proportion as I understood the language, I saw them from a new point of view.

Journal, March 5, 1858

I have never felt lonesome, or in the least oppressed by a sense of solitude, but once, and that was a few weeks after I came to the woods, when, for an hour, I doubted if the near neighborhood of man was not essential to a serene and healthy life. To be alone was something unpleasant. But I was at the same time conscious of a slight insanity in my mood, and seemed to foresee my recovery. In the midst of a gentle rain while these thoughts prevailed, I was suddenly sensible of such sweet and beneficent society in Nature, in the very pattering of the drops, and in every sound and sight across my house, an infinite and unaccountable friendliness all at once like an atmosphere sustaining me, as made the fancied advantages of human neighborhood insignificant, and I have never thought of them since. Every little pine needle expanded and swelled with sympathy and befriended me. I was so distinctly made aware of the presence of something kindred to me, even in scenes which we are accustomed to call wild and dreary, and also that the nearest of blood to me and humanest was not a person nor a villager, that I thought no place could ever be strange to me again.

We can never have enough of Nature;
we must be refreshed by the sight of
inexhaustible vigor, the wilderness with
its living and decaying trees, and the rain . . .

We can never have enough of Nature. We must be refreshed by the sight of inexhaustible vigor, vast and Titanic features, the seacoast with its wrecks, the wilderness with its living and its decaying trees, the thundercloud, and the rain which lasts three weeks and produces freshets. We need to witness our own limits transgressed, and some life pasturing freely where we never wander.

While these clouds and this somber drizzling weather shut all in, we two draw nearer and know one another. The gathering in of the clouds with the last rush and dying breath of the wind, and then the regular dripping of twigs and leaves the country o'er, the impression of inward comfort and sociableness, the drenched stubble and trees that drop beads on you as you pass, their dim outline seen through the rain on all sides drooping in sympathy with yourself. These are my undisputed territory.

Journal, March 30, 1840

Trees nurtured by rotting log.

Nature imitates all things in flowers;
they are at once the most beautiful
and the ugliest objects . . .

Nature imitates all things in flowers. They are at once the most beautiful and the ugliest objects, the most fragrant, and the most offensive to the nostrils.

Journal, June 13, 1852

I was inclined to think that the truest beauty was that which surrounded us but which we failed to discern, that the forms and colors which adorn our daily life, not seen afar in the horizon, are our fairest jewelry.

Journal, September 18, 1858

Black-eyed susan.

*I would rather watch the motions of these cows
in their pasture than wander to Europe or Asia . . .*

It is well to find your employment and amusement in
simple and homely things. These wear best and yield most.
I think I would rather watch the motions of these cows in
their pasture for a day, which I now see all headed one way
and slowly advancing, watch them and project their course
carefully on a chart, and report all their behavior faithfully,
than wander to Europe or Asia, and watch other motions
there; for it is only ourselves that we report in either case,
and perchance we shall report a more restless, worthless
self in the latter case than the former.

Journal, October 5, 1856

How well-behaved are cows! When they approach me
reclining in the shade, from curiosity, or to receive a whisp of
grass, or to share the shade, or to lick the dog held up, like a calf
— though just now they ran at him to toss him — they do not
obtrude. Their company is acceptable, for they can endure the
longest pause; they have not got to be entertained. They
occupy the most eligible lots in the town. I love to see some
pure white about them; they suggest the more neatness.

Journal, July 1, 1852

Farm cows in fog.

*I was self-appointed inspector of storms,
and did my duty faithfully; I have an eye
to the unfrequented corners of the farm . . .*

For many years I was self-appointed inspector of snow-storms and rainstorms, and did my duty faithfully; surveyor, if not of highways, then of forest paths and all across-lot routes, keeping them open, and ravines bridged and passable at all seasons, where the public heel had testified to their utility.

I have looked after the wild stock of the town, which give a faithful herdsman a good deal of trouble by leaping fences; and I have had an eye to the unfrequented nooks and corners of the farm; though I did not always know whether Jonas or Solomon worked in a particular field today; that was none of my business. I have watered the red huckleberry, the sand cherry and the nettle tree, the red pine and the black ash, the white grape and the yellow violet, which might have withered else in dry seasons.

Storm clouds over farm.

*F*lint's *Pond!* Such is the poverty of our nomenclature. What right had the unclean and stupid farmer, whose farm abutted on this sky water, whose shores he has ruthlessly laid bare, to give his name to it? Some skinflint, who loved better the reflecting surface of a dollar, or a bright cent, in which he could see his own brazen face; who regarded even the wild ducks which settled in it as trespassers; his fingers grown into crooked and horny talons from the long habit of grasping harpy-like; so it is not named for me. I go not there to see him nor to hear of him; who never *saw* it, who never bathed in it, who never loved it, who never protected it, who never spoke a good word for it, nor thanked God that He had made it. Rather let it be named from the fishes that swim in it, the wild fowl or quadrupeds which frequent it, the wild flowers which grow by its shores, or some wild man or child the thread of whose history is interwoven with its own; not from him who could show no title to it but the deed which a like-minded neighbor or legislature gave him — him who thought only of its money value; whose presence perchance cursed all the shore; who exhausted the land around it, and would fain have exhausted the waters within it; who regretted only that it was not English hay or cranberry meadow — there was nothing to redeem it, forsooth, in his eyes — and would have drained and sold it for the mud at its bottom. It did not turn his mill, and it was no *privilege* to him to behold it. I respect not his labors, his farm where everything has its price, who would carry the landscape, who would carry his God, to market, if he could get anything from him; who goes to market *for* his god as it is; on whose farm nothing grows free, whose fields bear no crops, whose meadows no flowers, whose trees no fruits, but dollars; who loves not the beauty of the fruits, whose fruits are not ripe for him till they are turned to dollars.

*Let the pond be named from the
fishes that swim in it, the wild fowl
or quadrupeds which frequent it, the
wild flowers which grow by its shores . . .*

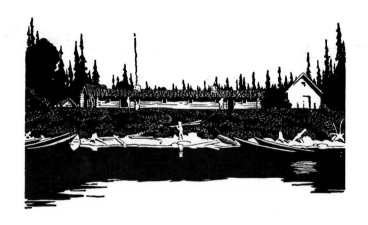

Our village life would stagnate
if it were not for the unexplored
forests and meadows which surround it;
we need the tonic of wilderness . . .

Our village life would stagnate if it were not for the unexplored forests and meadows which surround it. We need the tonic of wilderness—to wade sometimes in marshes where the bittern and the meadow-hen lurk, and hear the booming of the snipe; to smell the whispering sedge where only some wilder and more solitary fowl builds her nest, and the mink crawls with its belly close to the ground. At the same time that we are earnest to explore and learn all things, we require that all things be mysterious and unexplorable, that land and sea be infinitely wild, unsurveyed and unfathomed by us because unfathomable.

Waterfall and mountain ash berries.

Give me the poverty that enjoys true wealth; farmers are respectable and interesting to me in proportion as they are poor . . .

Give me the poverty that enjoys true wealth. Farmers are respectable and interesting to me in proportion as they are poor — poor farmers. A model farm! where the house stands like a fungus in a muck-heap, chambers for men, horses, oxen, and swine, cleansed and uncleansed, all contiguous to one another!

The farmer is endeavoring to solve the problem of a livelihood by a formula more complicated than the problem itself. To get his shoestrings he speculates in herds of cattle. With consummate skill he has set his trap with a hair springe to catch comfort and independence, and then, as he turned away, got his own leg into it. This is the reason he is poor; and for a similar reason we are all poor in respect to a thousand savage comforts, though surrounded by luxuries.

Old New England farm.

Morning mists.

I saw the pond throwing off its
nightly clothing of mists, which were,
like ghosts, stealthily withdrawing in
every direction into the woods . . .

For the first week, whenever I looked out on the pond it impressed me like a tarn high up on the side of a mountain, its bottom far above the surface of other lakes, and, as the sun arose, I saw it throwing off its nightly clothing of mist, and here and there, by degrees, its soft ripples or its smooth reflecting surface was revealed, while the mists, like ghosts, were stealthily withdrawing in every direction into the woods, as at the breaking up of some nocturnal conventicle. The very dew seemed to hang upon the trees later into the day than usual, as on the sides of mountains.

Commonly I rested an hour or two in the shade at noon, after planting, and ate my lunch, and read a little by a spring which was the source of a swamp and of a brook, oozing from under Brister's Hill, half a mile from my field. The approach to this was through a succession of descending grassy hollows, full of young pitch pines, into a larger wood about the swamp. There, in a very secluded and shaded spot, under a spreading white pine, there was yet a clean firm sward to sit on. I had dug out the spring and made a well of clear gray water, where I could dip up a pailful without roiling it, and thither I went for this purpose almost every day in mid-summer, when the pond was warmest. Thither too the woodcock led her brood, to probe the mud for worms, flying but a foot above them down the bank, while they ran in a troop beneath; but at last, spying me, she would leave her young and circle round and round me, nearer and nearer till within four or five feet, pretending broken wings and legs, to attract my attention, and get off her young, who would have already taken up their march, with faint wiry peep, single file through the swamp, as she directed. Or I heard the peep of the young when I could not see the parent bird. There too the turtle-doves sat over the spring, or fluttered from bough to bough of the soft white pines over my head; or the red squirrel, coursing down the nearest bough, was particularly familiar and inquisitive. You only need sit still long enough in some attractive spot in the woods that all its inhabitants may exhibit themselves to you by turns.

I rested an hour or two in the shade
at noon, after planting, and ate my lunch,
and read a little by a spring . . .

*I have my horizon bounded by woods
all to myself; for the most part it is as
solitary where I live as on the prairies;
I have a little world all to myself . . .*

For what reason have I this vast range and circuit, some square miles of unfrequented forest, for my privacy, abandoned to me by men? My nearest neighbor is a mile distant, and no house is visible from any place but the hilltops within half a mile of my own. I have my horizon bounded by woods all to myself; a distant view of the railroad where it touches the pond on the one hand, and of the fence which skirts the woodland road on the other. But for the most part it is as solitary where I live as on the prairies. It is as much Asia or Africa as New England. I have, as it were, my own sun and moon and stars, and a little world all to myself.

Ferns with pine and maple trunks.

*As Deliberately
as Nature*

Let us spend one day as deliberately as
Nature, and not be thrown off the track by
every nutshell and mosquito's wing that falls
on the rails. Let us rise early and fast, or break
fast, gently and without perturbation; let
company come and let company go, let the bells
ring and the children cry — determined to make a
day of it. Why should we knock under and go
with the stream? Let us not be upset and over-
whelmed in that terrible rapid and whirlpool called
a dinner, situated in the meridian shallows.
Weather this danger and you are safe, for the
rest of the way is downhill.

Blue elderberries.

*In some of Walden's coves grape vines had
run over the trees next the water and formed
bowers under which a boat could pass . . .*

When I first paddled a boat on Walden, it was completely surrounded by thick and lofty pine and oak woods, and in some of its coves grape vines had run over the trees next the water and formed bowers under which a boat could pass. The hills which form its shores are so steep, and the woods on them were so high, that, as you looked down from the west end, it had the appearance of an amphitheater for some kind of sylvan spectacle. I have spent many an hour, when I was younger, floating over its surface as the zephyr willed, having paddled my boat to the middle, and lying on my back across the seats, in a summer forenoon, dreaming awake, until I was aroused by the boat touching the sand, and I arose to see what shore my fates had impelled me to; days when idleness was the most attractive and productive industry.

Early fallen leaves and grasses.

In the intervals of a gentle rainstorm,
both air and water were perfectly still,
and the sky was overcast, and mid-afternoon
had all the serenity of evening . . .

This small lake was of most value as a neighbor in the intervals of a gentle rainstorm in August, when, both air and water being perfectly still, but the sky overcast, mid-afternoon had all the serenity of the evening, and the wood-thrush sang around, and was heard from shore to shore. A lake like this is never smoother than at such a time; and the clear portion of the air above it being shallow and darkened by clouds, the water, full of light and reflections, becomes a lower heaven itself so much the more important.

Once it chanced that I stood in the very abutment of a rainbow's arch, which filled the lower stratum of the atmosphere, tinging the grass and leaves around, and dazzling me as if I looked through colored crystal. It was a lake of rainbow light, in which, for a short while, I lived like a dolphin. If it had lasted longer it might have tinged my employments and life.

Amanita mushrooms.

Truth is as vivacious, and will
spread itself as fast, as the fungi . . .

Truth is as vivacious, and will spread itself as fast, as the fungi, which you can by no means annihilate with your heel, for their sporules are so infinitely numerous and subtle as to resemble "thin smoke, so light that they may be raised into an atmosphere, and dispersed in so many ways by the attraction of the sun, by insects, wind, elasticity, adhesion, etc.; that it is difficult to conceive a place from which they may be excluded."

Journal, November 5, 1840

As I was going up the hill, I was surprised to see rising above the June grass, near a walnut, a whitish object, like a stone with a white top, or a skunk erect, for it was black below. It was an enormous toadstool, or fungus, a sharply conical parasol in the form of a sugar loaf, slightly turned up at the edges, which were rent half an inch for every inch or two. . . . It was so delicate and fragile that its whole cap trembled at the least touch, and as I could not lay it down without injuring it, I was obliged to carry it home all the way in my hand, erect, while I paddled my boat with one hand. It was a wonder how its soft cone ever broke through the earth.

Journal, June 15, 1853

*It is a soothing employment to overlook
the pond and study the dimpling circles which
are incessantly inscribed on its surface . . .*

It is a soothing employment, on one of those fine days in the fall when all the warmth of the sun is fully appreciated, to sit on a stump on such a height as this, overlooking the pond, and study the dimpling circles which are incessantly inscribed on its otherwise invisible surface amid the reflected skies and trees. Over this great expanse there is no disturbance but it is thus at once gently smoothed away and assuaged, as, when a vase of water is jarred, the trembling circles seek the shore and all is smooth again. Not a fish can leap or an insect fall on the pond but it is thus reported in circling dimples, in lines of beauty, as it were the constant welling up of its fountain, the gentle pulsing of its life, the heaving of its breast.

Standing on the smooth sandy beach at the east end of the pond, in a calm September afternoon, when a slight haze makes the opposite shore line indistinct, I have seen whence came the expression, "the glassy surface of the lake." When you invert your head, it looks like a thread of finest gossamer stretched across the valley, and gleaming against the distant pine woods, separating one stratum of the atmosphere from another. You would think that you could walk dry under it to the opposite hills, and that the swallows which skim over might perch on it.

Time is but the stream I go a-fishing in;
I drink at it, but while I drink I see the
bottom and detect how shallow it is; its thin
current slides away, but eternity remains . . .

Time is but the stream I go a-fishing in. I drink at it; but while I drink I see the sandy bottom and detect how shallow it is. Its thin current slides away, but eternity remains. I would drink deeper; fish in the sky, whose bottom is pebbly with stars. I cannot count one. I know not the first letter of the alphabet. I have always been regretting that I was not as wise as the day I was born. The intellect is a cleaver; it discerns and rifts its way into the secret of things. I do not wish to be any more busy with my hands than is necessary. My head is hands and feet. I feel all my best faculties concentrated in it.

Browning ferns.

Sumac leaves.

*The sumach grew luxuriantly about the
house, pushing up through the embankment and
growing five or six feet the first season . . .*

The sumach (*rhus glabra*) grew luxuriantly about the house, pushing up through the embankment which I had made, and growing five or six feet the first season. Its broad pinnate tropical leaf was pleasant though strange to look on. The large buds, suddenly pushing out late in the spring from dry sticks which had seemed to be dead, developed themselves as by magic into graceful green and tender boughs, an inch in diameter....

I suspect that I know on what the brilliancy of the autumnal tints will depend. On the greater or less drought of the summer. If the drought has been uncommonly severe, as this year, I should think it would so far destroy the vitality of the leaf that it would attain only to a dull, dead color in autumn; that to become brilliant in autumn, the plant should be full of sap and vigor to the last.

Journal, September 25, 1854

It is indeed a golden autumn; these days are enough to make the reputation of any climate . . .

It is indeed a golden autumn. These ten days are enough to make the reputation of any climate. A tradition of these days might be handed down to posterity. They deserve a notice in history, in the history of Concord. All kinds of crudities have a chance to get ripe this year. Was there ever such an autumn? . . .

Sat in the old pasture beyond the Corner Spring woods to look at that pine wood now at the height of its change, pitch and white. Their change produces a very singular and pleasing effect. They are regularly parti-colored. The last year's leaves about a foot beneath the extremities of the twigs on all sides, now changed and ready to fall, have their period of brightness as well as broader leaves. They are a clear yellow, contrasting with the fresh and liquid green of the terminal plumes, or this year's leaves. These quite distinct colors are regularly and equally distributed over the whole tree. You have the warmth of the yellow and the coolness of the green. So it should be with our own maturity, not yellow to the very extremity of our shoots, but youthful and untried green ever putting forth afresh at the extremities, foretelling a maturity as yet unknown. The ripe leaves fall to the ground, and become nutriment for the green ones which still aspire to heaven. In the fall of the leaf there is no fruit, there is no true maturity, neither in our science and wisdom.

Journal, October 14, 1857

Maple and hazelnut leaves accent a spruce.

The loon maneuvered so cunningly that I could not get near him; each time, when he came to the surface, he coolly surveyed the water . . .

As I was paddling along the north shore one very calm October afternoon, for such days especially they settle onto the lakes, like the milkweed down, having looked in vain over the pond for a loon, suddenly one, sailing out from the shore toward the middle a few rods in front of me, set up his wild laugh and betrayed himself. I pursued with a paddle and he dived, but when he came up I was nearer than before. He dived again, but I miscalculated the direction he would take, and we were fifty rods apart when he came to the surface this time, for I had helped to widen the interval; and again he laughed long and loud, and with more reason than before. He maneuvered so cunningly that I could not get within half a dozen rods of him. Each time, when he came to the surface, turning his head this way and that, he coolly surveyed the water and the land, and apparently chose his course so that he might come up where there was the widest expanse of water and at the greatest distance from the boat. It was surprising how quickly he made up his mind and put his resolve into execution. He led me at once to the widest part of the pond, and could not be driven from it. While he was thinking one thing in his brain, I was endeavoring to divine his thoughts in mine. It was a pretty game, played on the smooth surface of the pond, a man against a loon.

In the fall the loon (*Colymbus glacialis*) came, as usual, to moult and bathe in the pond, making the woods ring with his wild laughter before I had risen. At rumor of his arrival all the Mill-dam sportsmen are on the alert, in gigs and on foot, two by two and three by three, with patent rifles and conical balls and spyglasses. They come rustling through the woods like autumn leaves, at least ten men to one loon. Some station themselves on this side of the pond, some on that, for the poor bird cannot be omnipresent; if he dive here he must come up there. But now the kind October wind rises, rustling the leaves and rippling the surface of the water, so that no loon can be heard or seen, though his foes sweep the pond with spyglasses, and make the woods resound with their discharges. The waves generously rise and dash angrily, taking sides with all waterfowl, and our sportsmen must beat a retreat to town and shop and unfinished jobs.

Country road.

*I find it wholesome to be alone the
greater part of the time; to be in company
is soon wearisome and dissipating . . .*

I find it wholesome to be alone the greater part of the time. To be in company, even with the best, is soon wearisome and dissipating. I love to be alone. I never found the companion that was so companionable as solitude. We are for the most part more lonely when we go abroad among men than when we stay in our chambers. A man thinking or working is always alone, let him be where he will. Solitude is not measured by the miles of space that intervene between a man and his fellows.

By my intimacy with nature I find myself withdrawn from man. My interest in the sun and the moon, in the morning and the evening, compels me to solitude.

Journal, July 26, 1852

Purple grapes.

I went a-graping to the river meadows,
and loaded myself with clusters more precious
for their beauty and fragrance than for food . . .

In October I went a-graping to the river meadows, and loaded myself with clusters more precious for their beauty and fragrance than for food. There too I admired, though I did not gather, the cranberries, small waxen gems, pendants of the meadow grass, pearly and red. . . .

The grapes would no doubt be riper a week hence, but I am compelled to go now before the vines are stripped. I partly smell them out. I pluck splendid great bunches of the purple ones, with a rich bloom on them and the purple glowing through it like a fire; large red ones, also, with light dots, and some clear green. Sometimes I crawl under low and thick bowers, where they have run over the alders only four or five feet high, and see the grapes hanging from a hollow hemisphere of leaves over my head. At other times I see them dark-purple or black against the silver undersides of the leaves, high overhead where they run over birches or maples, and either climb or pull them down to pluck them.

Journal, September 8, 1854

*I look where the trees glow yellow
and scarlet through the green, like fires
just kindled at the base of the trees . . .*

Standing on the railroad, I look across the pond to Pine Hill, where the outside trees, and the shrubs scattered generally through the wood, glow yellow and scarlet through the green, like fires just kindled at the base of the trees, a general conflagration just fairly under way, soon to envelop every tree. The hillside forest is all aglow along its edge, and in all its cracks and fissures, and soon the flames will leap upwards to the tops of the tallest trees.

Journal, October 3, 1858

There is commonly sufficient space about us. Our horizon is never quite at our elbows. The thick wood is not just at our door, nor the pond, but somewhat is always clearing, familiar and worn by us, appropriated and fenced in some way, and reclaimed from Nature.

Sugar maple leaves.

*A lake is the landscape's most beautiful
and expressive feature; it is the earth's
eye, and the trees next the shore are the
slender eyelashes which fringe it . . .*

A lake is the landscape's most beautiful and expressive feature. It is earth's eye; looking into which the beholder measures the depth of his own nature. The fluviatile trees next the shore are the slender eyelashes which fringe it, and the wooded hills and cliffs around are its overhanging brows.

The forest has never so good a setting, nor is so distinctly beautiful, as when seen from the middle of a small lake amid hills which rise from the water's edge; for the water in which it is reflected not only makes the best foreground in such a case, but, with its winding shore, the most natural and agreeable boundary to it.

Autumn shoreline.

Already I had seen small maples turned scarlet across the pond, where the white stems of aspens diverged; many a tale their color told . . .

Already, by the first of September, I had seen two or three small maples turned scarlet across the pond, beneath where the white stems of three aspens diverged, at the point of a promontory, next the water. Ah, many a tale their color told! And gradually from week to week the character of each tree came out, and it admired itself reflected in the smooth mirror of the lake. Each morning the manager of this gallery substituted some new picture, distinguished by more brilliant or harmonious coloring, for the old upon the walls.

The intense brilliancy of the red-ripe maples scattered here and there in the midst of the green oaks and hickories on the hilly shore of Walden is quite charming. They are unexpectedly and incredibly brilliant, especially on the western shore and close to the water's edge, where, alternating with yellow branches and poplars and green oaks, they remind me of a line of soldiers, redcoats and riflemen in green mixed together.

Journal, September 29, 1851

Maple leaves and birch trunks.

My heart leaps into my mouth at the sound of the wind in the woods. I, whose life was but yesterday so desultory and shallow, suddenly recover my spirits, my spirituality, through my hearing. I see a goldfinch go twittering through the still, louring day, and am reminded of the peeping flocks which will soon herald the thoughtful season. Ah! if I could so live that there should be no desultory moment in all my life! that in the trivial season, when small fruits are ripe, my fruits might be ripe also! that I could match nature always with my moods! that in each season when some part of nature especially flourishes, then a corresponding part of me may not fail to flourish! Ah, I would walk, I would sit and sleep, with natural piety! What if I could pray aloud or to myself as I went along by the brook-sides a cheerful prayer like the birds! For joy I could embrace the earth; I shall delight to be buried in it.

Journal, August 17, 1851

How beautiful the leaves go to their
graves! How gently lay themselves down and
turn to mould! Painted of a thousand hues and
fit to make the beds of us living . . .

How pleasant to walk over beds of these fresh, crisp, and rustling fallen leaves — young hyson, green tea, clean, crisp, and wholesome! How beautiful they go to their graves! how gently lay themselves down and turn to mould! — painted of a thousand hues and fit to make the beds of us living.... How they are mixed up, all species — oak and maple and chestnut and birch! They are about to add a leaf's breadth to the depth of the soil. We are all the richer for their decay.

Journal, October 20, 1853

Drizzling, misty showers still, with a little misty sunshine at intervals. The trees have lost many of their leaves in the last twenty-four hours. The sun has got so low that it will do to let his rays in on the earth; the cattle do not need their shade now, nor men. Warmth is more desirable than shade.

Journal, October 13, 1851

Red maple leaves.

Spruce-fir-aspen forest.

Lately we had a leafy wilderness;
now bare twigs begin to prevail, and it
begins to appear what is evergreen . . .

Nature has many scenes to exhibit, and constantly draws a curtain over this part or that. She is constantly repainting the landscape and all surfaces, dressing up some scene for our entertainment. Lately we had a leafy wilderness; now bare twigs begin to prevail, and soon she will surprise us with a mantle of snow. Some green she thinks so good for our eyes that, like blue, she never banishes it entirely from our eyes, but has created evergreens.

Journal, November 8, 1858

Now that the grass is withered and the leaves are withered or fallen, it begins to appear what is evergreen: the partridge [-berry] and checkerberry, and wintergreen leaves even, are more conspicuous.

Journal, November 19, 1850

Trees reflected in water.

At the end of a rainstorm, when the sky was still overcast, the pond was remarkably smooth; the slight undulations from my boat gave a ribbed appearance to the reflections . . .

One November afternoon, in the calm at the end of a rainstorm of several days' duration, when the sky was still completely overcast and the air was full of mist, I observed that the pond was remarkably smooth, so that it was difficult to distinguish its surface; though it no longer reflected the bright tints of October, but the somber November colors of the surrounding hills. Though I passed over it as gently as possible, the slight undulations produced by my boat extended almost as far as I could see, and gave a ribbed appearance to the reflections.

Wisdom
Does Not Despair

The mass of men lead lives of quiet desperation. What is called resignation is confirmed desperation. From the desperate city you go into the desperate country, and have to console yourself with the bravery of minks and muskrats. A stereotyped but unconscious despair is concealed even under what are called the games and amusements of mankind. There is no play in them, for this comes after work. But it is characteristic of wisdom not to do desperate things.

Canada geese.

Each day the geese came splashing
in with a clangor and whistling of wings;
I heard the tread of geese on the dry
leaves in the woods behind my dwelling . . .

At length the winter set in in good earnest, just as I had finished plastering, and the wind began to howl around the house as if it had not had permission to do so till then. Night after night the geese came lumbering in in the dark with a clangor and a whistling of wings, even after the ground was covered with snow, some to alight in Walden, and some flying low over the woods toward Fair Haven, bound for Mexico. Several times, when returning from the village at ten or eleven o'clock at night, I heard the tread of a flock of geese, or else ducks, on the dry leaves in the woods by a pond-hole behind my dwelling, where they had come up to feed, and the faint honk or quack of their leader as they hurried off.

For hours, in fall days, I watched the ducks cunningly tack and veer and hold the middle of the pond, far from the sportsmen; tricks which they will have less need to practice in Louisiana bayous. When compelled to rise they would sometimes circle round and round and over the pond at a considerable height, from which they could easily see to other ponds and the river, like black motes in the sky; and, when I thought they had gone off thither long since, they would settle down by a slanting flight of a quarter of a mile onto a distant part which was left free; but what beside safety they got by sailing in the middle of Walden I do not know, unless they love its water for the same reason that I do.

*This is a delicious evening, when the
whole body is one sense, and imbibes delight
through every pore; I go and come with a strange
liberty in Nature, a part of herself . . .*

This is a delicious evening, when the whole body is one
sense, and imbibes delight through every pore. I go and
come with a strange liberty in Nature, a part of herself. As I
walk along the stony shore of the pond in my shirt sleeves,
though it is cool as well as cloudy and windy, and I see
nothing special to attract me, all the elements are unusually
congenial to me. The bullfrogs trump to usher in the night,
and the note of the whippoorwill is borne on the rippling
wind from over the water. Sympathy with the fluttering
alder and poplar leaves almost takes away my breath; yet,
like the lake, my serenity is rippled but not ruffled. These
small waves raised by the evening wind are as remote from
storm as the smooth reflecting surface. Though it is now
dark, the wind still blows and roars in the wood, the waves
still dash, and some creatures lull the rest with their notes.

Flock of geese at sunset.

Frost on pine needles.

*Early in the morning every pine needle
was covered with a frosty sheath, but
soon after sunrise it was all gone . . .*

The winter morning is the time to see in perfection the
woods and shrubs wearing their snowy and frosty dress.
Even he who visits them half an hour after sunrise will
have lost some of their most delicate and fleeting beauties.
The trees wear their morning burden but coarsely after mid-
day, and it no longer expresses the character of the tree. I
observed that early in the morning every pine needle was
covered with a frosty sheath, but soon after sunrise it was
all gone. You walk in the pitch-pine woods as under a pent-
house. The stems and branches of the trees look black by
contrast. You wander zigzag through the aisles of the wood,
where stillness and twilight reign. I do not know but a pine
wood is as substantial and as memorable a fact as a friend.
I am more sure to come away from it cheered than from
those who are nearest to being my friends.

Journal, December 17, 1851

The first ice is especially interesting and perfect, being hard, dark and transparent . . .

The pond had in the meanwhile skimmed over in the shadiest and shallowest coves, some days or even weeks before the general freezing. The first ice is especially interesting and perfect, being hard, dark, and transparent, and affords the best opportunity that ever offers for examining the bottom where it is shallow; for you can lie at your length on ice only an inch thick, like a skater insect on the surface of the water, and study the bottom at your leisure, only two or three inches distant, like a picture behind a glass, and the water is necessarily always smooth then. . . . If you examine it closely the morning after it freezes, you find that the greater part of the bubbles, which at first appeared to be within it, are against its under surface, and that more are continually rising from the bottom; while the ice is as yet comparatively solid and dark, that is, you see the water through it. These bubbles are from an eightieth to an eighth of an inch in diameter, very clear and beautiful, and you see your face reflected in them through the ice.

Early ice formation.

Long-eared owls.

I rejoice that there are owls; let
them do the idiotic and maniacal hooting
for men; they represent a stark twilight
and unsatisfied thoughts which all have . . .

J rejoice that there are owls. Let them do the idiotic and maniacal hooting for men. It is a sound admirably suited to swamps and twilight woods which no day illustrates, suggesting a vast and undeveloped nature which men have not recognized. They represent the stark twilight and unsatisfied thoughts which all have. All day the sun has shone on the surface of some savage swamp, where the single spruce stands hung with usnea lichens, and small hawks circulate above, and the chickadee lisps amid the evergreens, and the partridge and the rabbit skulk beneath; but now a more dismal and fitting day dawns, and a different race of creatures awakes to express the meaning of Nature there.

The snow surrounded me suddenly with the scenery of winter; I withdrew yet farther into my shell, and endeavored to keep a fire within my house and within my breast . . .

The snow had already covered the ground since the 25th of November, and surrounded me suddenly with the scenery of winter. I withdrew yet farther into my shell, and endeavored to keep a bright fire both within my house and within my breast. My employment out of doors now was to collect the dead wood in the forest, bringing it in my hands or on my shoulders, or sometimes trailing a dead pine tree under each arm to my shed. An old forest fence which had seen its best days was a great haul for me. I sacrificed it to Vulcan, for it was past serving the god Terminus.

My home is as much of nature as my heart embraces. If I only warm my house, then is that only my home. But if I sympathize with the heats and colds, the sounds and silence of nature, and share the repose and equanimity that reign around me in the fields, then are they my house, as much as if the kettle sang and fagots crackled, and the clock ticked on the wall.

Journal, December 20, 1840

Winter grasses.

*I frequently tramped eight or ten miles
through the deepest snow to keep an appointment
with a beech tree, or a yellow birch . . .*

But no weather interfered fatally with my walks, or rather my going abroad, for I frequently tramped eight or ten miles through the deepest snow to keep an appointment with a beech tree, or a yellow birch, or an old acquaintance among the pines; when the ice and snow causing their limbs to droop, and so sharpening their tops, had changed the pines into fir trees; wading to the tops of the highest hills when the snow was nearly two feet deep on a level, and shaking down another snowstorm on my head at every step; or sometimes creeping and floundering thither on my hands and knees, when the hunters had gone into winter quarters.

Squirrels and wild mice disputed for my store of nuts. There were scores of pitch pines around my house, from one to four inches in diameter, which had been gnawed by mice the previous winter — a Norwegian winter for them, for the snow lay long and deep, and they were obliged to mix a large proportion of pine bark with their other diet. These trees were alive and apparently flourishing at midsummer, and many of them had grown a foot, though completely girdled; but after another winter such were without exception dead. It is remarkable that a single mouse should thus be allowed a whole pine tree for its dinner, gnawing round instead of up and down it; but perhaps it is necessary in order to thin these trees, which are wont to grow up densely.

*When the ground was not quite covered
by snow, the partridges came out of the
woods morning and evening to feed there . . .*

When the ground was not yet quite covered, and again near the end of winter, when the snow was melted on my south hillside and about my woodpile, the partridges came out of the woods morning and evening to feed there. Whichever side you walk in the woods the partridge bursts away on whirring wings, jarring the snow from the dry leaves and twigs on high, which comes sifting down in the sunbeams like golden dusts, for this brave bird is not to be scared by winter. It is frequently covered up by drifts, and, it is said, "sometimes plunges from on wing into the soft snow, where it remains concealed for a day or two." I used to start them in the open land also, where they had come out of the woods at sunset to "bud" the wild apple trees. They will come regularly every evening to particular trees, where the cunning sportsman lies in wait for them, and the distant orchards next the woods suffer thus not a little. I am glad that the partridge gets fed, at any rate. It is Nature's own bird which lives on buds and diet-drink.

Pheasants feeding in field.

Winter stream.

What beauty in the running brooks! What life!
What society! The cold is merely superficial;
it is still summer at the core far within . . .

Perhaps what most moves us in winter is some reminiscence of far-off summer. How we leap by the side of the open brooks! What beauty in the running brooks! What life! What society! The cold is merely superficial; it is summer still at the core, far, far within.

Journal, January 12, 1855

Nature is moderate, and loves degrees. Winter is not all white and cere. Some trees are evergreen to cheer us, and on the forest floor our eyes do not fall on sere brown leaves alone, but some evergreen shrubs are placed there to relieve the eye. Mountain laurel, lambkill, checkerberry, wintergreen, etc., keep up the semblance of summer still.

Journal, November 17, 1858

*The elements abetted me in making a
path through the deepest snow in the woods,
for the wind blew leaves into my tracks . . .*

I weathered some merry snowstorms, and spent some cheerful winter evenings by my fireside, while the snow whirled wildly without, and even the hooting of the owl was hushed. For many weeks I met no one in my walks but those who came occasionally to cut wood and sled it to the village. The elements, however, abetted me in making a path through the deepest snow in the woods, for when I had once gone through, the wind blew the oak leaves into my tracks, where they lodged, and by absorbing the rays of the sun melted the snow, and so not only made a dry bed for my feet, but in the night their dark line was my guide.

Sometimes I heard the foxes as they ranged over the snow crust, in moonlight nights, in search of a partridge or other game, barking raggedly and demoniacally like forest dogs, as if laboring with some anxiety, or seeking expression, struggling for light and to be dogs outright and run freely in the streets....

Oats.

It was pleasant to compare the first signs
of the infant year with the beauty of the
withered vegetation which withstood the winter
— unexhausted granaries which serve the birds . . .

When the ground was partially bare of snow, and a few warm days had dried its surface somewhat, it was pleasant to compare the first tender signs of the infant year just peeping forth with the stately beauty of the withered vegetation which had withstood the winter—life-everlasting, goldenrods, pinweeds, and graceful wild grasses, more obvious and interesting frequently than in summer even, as if their beauty was not ripe till then; even cotton-grass, cat-tails, mulleins, johnswort, hard-hack, meadow-sweet, and other strong-stemmed plants, those unexhausted granaries which entertain the earliest birds—decent weeds, at least, which widowed Nature wears.

*Seeing the Moonlight
Amid the Mountains*

It is remarkable how easily and insensibly we fall into a particular route, and make a beaten track for ourselves. I had not lived there for a week before my feet wore a path from my door to the pond-side; and though it is five or six years since I trod it, it is still quite distinct. It is true, I fear, that others may have fallen into it, and so helped to keep it open. The surface of the earth is soft and impressionable by the feet of men; and so with the paths which the mind travels. How worn and dusty, then, must be the highways of the world, how deep the ruts of tradition and conformity! I did not wish to take a cabin passage, but rather to go before the mast and on the deck of the world, for there I could best see the moonlight amid the mountains. I do not wish to go below now.

Early in May, the trees, just putting out amidst the pine woods around the pond, imparted a brightness like sunshine to the landscape . . .

Early in May, the oaks, hickories, maples and other trees, just putting out amidst the pine woods around the pond, imparted a brightness like sunshine to the landscape, especially in cloudy days, as if the sun were breaking through mists and shining faintly on the hillsides here and there.

It is surprising how the earth on south banks begins to show some greenness in its russet cheeks in this rain and fog — a precious emerald-green tinge, almost like a green mildew, the growth of the night, a green blush suffusing her cheek, heralded by twittering birds. This sight is no less interesting than the corresponding bloom and ripe blush of the fall. How encouraging to perceive again that faint tinge of green spreading amid the russet on earth's cheeks! I revive with Nature. Her victory is mine. This is my jewelry.

Journal, April 3, 1856

Dogwood in bloom.

Canada geese.

*For a week I heard the circling groping
clangor of some solitary goose in the foggy
mornings, seeking its companion . . .*

For a week I heard the circling groping clangor of some
solitary goose in the foggy mornings, seeking its companion,
and still peopling the woods with the sound of a larger life
than they could sustain. In April the pigeons were seen
again flying express in small flocks, and in due time I heard
the martins twittering over my clearing, though it had not
seemed that the township contained so many that it could
afford me any, and I fancied that they were peculiarly of the
ancient race that dwelt in hollow trees ere white men came.
In almost all climes the tortoise and the frog are among the
precursors and heralds of this season, and birds fly with
song and glancing plumage, and plant spring and bloom,
and winds blow, to correct this slight oscillation of the poles
and preserve the equilibrium of Nature.

As every season seems best to us in its turn, so the
coming in of spring is like the creation of Cosmos out of
Chaos and the realization of the Golden Age.

*I am on the alert for the first signs
of spring, to hear the chance note of some
arriving bird, or the squirrel's chirp . . .*

One attraction in coming to the woods to live was that I should have leisure and opportunity to see the Spring come in. The ice in the pond at length begins to be honeycombed, and I can set my heel in it as I walk. Fogs and rains and warmer suns are gradually melting the snow; the days have grown sensibly longer; and I see how I shall get through the winter without adding to my woodpile, for large fires are no longer necessary. I am on the alert for the first signs of spring, to hear the chance note of some arriving bird, or the striped squirrel's chirp, for his stores must be now nearly exhausted, or see the woodchuck venture out of his winter quarters. On the 13th of March, after I had heard the bluebird, song-sparrow, and the redwing, the ice was still nearly a foot thick. As the weather grew warmer it was not sensibly worn away by the water, nor broken up and floated off as in rivers, but, though it was completely melted for half a rod in width about the shore, the middle was merely honeycombed and saturated with water, so that you could put your foot through it when six inches thick; but by the next day evening, after a warm rain followed by fog, it would have wholly disappeared, all gone off with the fog, spirited away.

The first sparrow of spring! The year beginning with younger hope than ever! The faint silvery warblings heard over the partially bare and moist fields from the bluebird, the song-sparrow, and the redwing, as if the last flakes of winter tinkled as they fell! What at such a time are histories, chronologies, traditions, and all written revelations? The brooks sing carols and glees to the spring. The marsh-hawk sailing low over the meadow is already seeking the first slimy life that awakes. The sinking sound of melting snow is heard in all dells, and the ice dissolves apace in the ponds.

Female ruby-throated hummingbird on nest.

*I found myself suddenly neighbor to the
birds by having caged myself near them . . .*

The only house I had been the owner of before, if I
except a boat, was a tent, which I used occasionally when
making excursions in the summer, and this is still rolled up
in my garret; but the boat, after passing from hand to hand,
has gone down the stream of time. With this more
substantial shelter about me, I had made some progress
toward settling in the world. This frame, so slightly clad,
was a sort of crystallization around me, and reacted on the
builder. It was suggestive somewhat as a picture in outlines.
I did not need to go outdoors to take the air, for the
atmosphere within had lost none of its freshness. It was not
so much within doors as behind a door where I sat, even in
the rainiest weather. The Harivansa says, "An abode
without birds is like a meat without seasoning." Such was
not my abode, for I found myself suddenly neighbor to the
birds; not by having imprisoned one, but having caged
myself near them. I was not only nearer to some of those
which commonly frequent the garden and the orchard, but
to those wilder and more thrilling songsters of the forest
which never, or rarely, serenade a villager — the wood-
thrush, the veery, the scarlet tanager, the field sparrow, the
whippoorwill, and many others.

Butterflies of various colors are now more abundant than I have ever seen them before; they presented a very lifesome scene . . .

Butterflies of various colors are now more abundant than I have ever seen them before, especially the small reddish or coppery ones. I counted ten yesterday on a single *Seriocarpus conyzoides* [aster]. They were in a single harmony with the plant, as if they made a part of it. The insect that comes after the honey or pollen of a plant is necessary to it and in one sense makes a part of it. Being constantly in motion and, as they moved, opening and closing their wings to preserve their balances, they presented a very lifesome scene.

Journal, July 29, 1853

The forenoon is fuller of light. The butterflies on the flowers look like other and frequently larger flowers themselves.

Journal, July 21, 1851

Gray hairstreak butterfly on wallflower.

Checker flower.

*With what a variety of colors we
are entertained! The eyes feast on the
colors of flowers as on tidbits . . .*

With what a variety of colors we are entertained! Yet most colors are rare or in small doses, presented to us as a condiment or spice; much of green, blue, black, and white, but of yellow and the different shades of red, far less. The eyes feast on the colors of flowers as on tidbits.

Journal, June 1, 1853

Methinks this is the first of the dog-days. The air in the distance has a peculiar blue mistiness, or furnace-like look. . . . The season of fruits is arrived. The dog's-bane has a pretty, delicate bell-like flower. . . . These are among our pleasantest woods — open, level, with blackberry vines interspersed and flowers, as lady's-slippers, earlier, and pinks on the outskirts.

Journal, July 16, 1851

We are not chiefly interested in birds and insects, for example, as they are ornamental to the earth and cheering to man, but we spare the lives of the former only on the condition that they eat more grubs than they do cherries, and the only account of the insects which the State encourages is of the "Insects *Injurious* to Vegetation." We too admit both a good and a bad spirit, but we worship chiefly the bad spirit, whom we fear. We do not think first of the good but of the harm things will do us.

Journal, May 1, 1859

I see somewhat more of my own kith
and kin in the lichens on the rocks than
in any books; it seems as if mine
were a particularly wild nature . . .

J seem to see somewhat more of my own kith and kin in the lichens on the rocks than in any books. It does seem as if mine were a particularly wild nature, which so yearns toward all wildness. I know of no redeeming qualities in me but a sincere love for some things....

Journal, December 15, 1841

The scenery of Walden is on a humble scale, and, though very beautiful, does not approach to grandeur, nor can it much concern one who has not long frequented it or lived by its shore....

Dead oak trunk and boulders with lichens.

The Miracle
of Change

I think we may safely trust a good deal more than we do. . . . How vigilant we are! determined not to live by faith if we can avoid it; all the day long on the alert, at night we unwillingly say our prayers and commit ourselves to uncertainties. So thoroughly and sincerely we are compelled to live, reverencing our life, and denying the possibility of change. This is the only way, we say; but there are as many ways as there can be drawn radii from one center. All change is a miracle to contemplate; but it is a miracle which is taking place every instant.

*How many mornings, summer and winter,
before yet any neighbor was stirring about
his business, have I been about mine . . .*

To anticipate, not the sunrise and the dawn merely, but, if possible, Nature herself! How many mornings, summer and winter, before yet any neighbor was stirring about his business, have I been about mine.

It is surprising how much room there is in nature — if a man will follow his proper path. In these broad fields, in these extensive woods, on this stretching river, I never meet a walker. Passing behind the farmhouses, I see no man out. Perhaps I do not meet so many men as I should have met three centuries ago, when the Indian hunter roamed these woods. I enjoy the retirement and solitude of an early settler. Men have cleared some of the earth, which no doubt is an advantage to the walker.

Journal, January 26, 1853

Farm geese at dawn.

Now I yearn for one of those old, meandering, dry, uninhabited roads, which lead away from towns, which lead us away from temptation, which conduct to the outside of earth, over its uppermost crust; where you may forget in what country you are traveling; where no farmer can complain that you are treading down his grass, no gentlemen who has recently constructed a seat in the country that you are trespassing; on which you can go off at half-cock and wave adieu to the village; along which you may travel like a pilgrim, going nowhither; where travelers are not too often to be met; where my spirit is free; where the walls and fences are not cared for; where your head is more in heaven than your feet are on earth. . . . I cannot walk habitually in those ways that are liable to be mended; for sure it was the devil only that wore them. Never by the heel of thinkers (of thought) were they worn; the zephyrs could repair that damage. The saunterer wears out no road, even though he travel on it, and therefore should pay no highway, or rather, *low* way, tax. He may be taxed to construct a higher way than men travel. A way which no geese defile, nor hiss along it, but only sometimes their wild brethren fly far overhead; which the kingbird and the swallow twitter over, and the song sparrow sings on its rails; where the small red butterfly is at home on the yarrow, and no boys threaten it with imprisoning hat. There I can walk and stalk and pace and plod.

Journal, July 21, 1851

I yearn for one of those old,
meandering roads which lead us away
from town, away from temptation . . .

*Nature has no human inhabitant who
appreciates her; she flourishes most alone . . .*

Nature has no human inhabitant who appreciates her. The birds with their plumage and their notes are in harmony with the flowers, but what youth or maiden conspires with the wild luxuriant beauty of Nature? She flourishes most alone, far from the towns where they reside.

When the farmer cleans out his ditches, I mourn the loss of many a flower which he calls a weed. The main charm about the lower road, just beyond the bridge, to me has been in the little grove of locusts, sallows, birches, etc., which has sprung up on the bank as you rise the hill. Yesterday I saw a man who is building a house nearby cutting them down. Finding he was going to cut them all, I said if I were in his place I would not have them cut for a hundred dollars. "Why," said he, "they are nothing but a parcel of prickly bushes and are not worth anything. I'm going to build a new wall here." And so to ornament the approach to his house he substituted a bare ugly wall for an interesting grove.

Journal, April 10, 1853

Turk's cap lily.

Many a forenoon I have stolen away,
preferring to spend the most valued part of
day, for I was rich in sunny hours and
summer days, and spent them lavishly . . .

Many a forenoon have I stolen away, preferring to spend thus the most valued part of the day; for I was rich, if not in money, in sunny hours and summer days, and spent them lavishly; nor do I regret that I did not waste more of them in the workshop or the teacher's desk.

In warm evenings I frequently sat in the boat playing the flute, and saw the perch, which I seem to have charmed, hovering around me, and the moon traveling over the ribbed bottom, which was strewed with the wrecks of the forest.

Waterfalls and moss-covered rocks.

It is well to have some water in your neighborhood, to give buoyancy to and float the earth. . . . When I looked across the pond from this peak toward the Sudbury meadows, which in time of flood I distinguished elevated perhaps by a mirage in their seething valley, like a coin in a basin, all the earth beyond the pond appeared like a thin crust insulated and floated even by this small sheet of intervening water, and I was reminded that this on which I dwelt was but dry land.

It is worth the while to have had a cloudy, even a stormy, day for an excursion, if only that you are out at the clearing up. The beauty of the landscape is greater, not only by reason of the contrast with its recent lowering aspect, but because of the greater freshness and purity of the air and of vegetation, and of the repressed and so recruited spirits of the beholder. Sunshine is nothing to be observed or described, but when it is seen in patches on the hillsides, or suddenly bursts forth with splendor at the end of a storm. I derive pleasure now from the shadows of the clouds diversifying the sunshine on the hills, where lately all was shadow. The spirits of the cows at pasture on this very hillside appear excited. They are restless from a kind of joy, and are not content with feeding. The weedy shore is suddenly blotted out by this rise of waters.

Journal, August 31, 1852

When I looked across the pond
from this peak, all the earth beyond
the pool appeared like a thin crust . . .

Underside of black and yellow argiope spider.

*I am no more lonely than the Mill
Brook, or a weathercock, or the North Star,
or the first spider in a new house . . .*

I am no more lonely than the loon in the pond that laughs so loud, or than Walden Pond itself. What company has that lonely lake, I pray! And yet it has not the blue devils, but the blue angels in it, in the azure tint of its waters. The sun is alone, except in thick weather, when there sometimes appear to be two, but one is a mock sun. God is alone—but the devil, he is far from being alone; he sees a great deal of company; he is legion. I am no more lonely than a single mullein or dandelion in a pasture, or a bean leaf, or sorrel, or a horsefly, or a bumblebee. I am no more lonely than the Mill Brook, or a weathercock, or the North Star, or the south wind, or an April shower, or a January thaw, or the first spider in a new house.

I looked between and over the near green hills to some distant and higher ones in the horizon, tinged with blue . . .

From a hilltop near by, where the wood had been recently cut off, there was a pleasing vista southward across the pond, through a wide indentation in the hills which form the shore there, where their opposite sides sloping toward each other suggested a stream flowing out in that direction through a wooded valley, but stream there was none. That way I looked between and over the near green hills to some distant and higher ones in the horizon, tinged with blue. Indeed, by standing on tiptoe I could catch a glimpse of some of the peaks of the still bluer and more distant mountain ranges in the northwest....

Mountain pasture.

An old man who used to frequent this pond nearly sixty years ago, when it was dark with surrounding forests, tells me that in those days he sometimes saw it all alive with ducks and other water fowl, and that there were many eagles about it. He came here a-fishing, and used an old log canoe which he found on the shore. It was made of two white-pine logs dug out and pinned together, and was cut off square at the ends. It was very clumsy, but lasted a great many years before it became waterlogged and perhaps sank to the bottom. He did not know whose it was; it belonged to the pond.

*The real attractions of the Hollowell
farm were, to me, the gray color and
ruinous state of the house and barn . . .*

The real attractions of the Hollowell farm, to me, were: its complete retirement, being about two miles from the village, half a mile from the nearest neighbor, and separated from the highway by a broad field; its bounding on the river, which the owner said protected it by its fogs from frosts in the spring, though that was nothing to me; the gray color and ruinous state of the house and barn, and the dilapidated fences, which put such an interval between me and the last occupant; the hollow and lichen-covered apple trees, gnawed by rabbits, showing what kind of neighbors I should have; but above all, the recollection I had of it from my earliest voyages up the river, when the house was concealed behind a dense grove of red maples, through which I heard the house-dog bark. I was in haste to buy it, before the proprietor finished getting out some rocks, cutting down the hollow apple trees, and grubbing up some young birches which had sprung up in the pasture, or, in short, had made any more of his improvements.

Old barn, sheep, rooster and birches.

How plain, wholesome and earthy are the colors of quadrupeds! The commonest is the tawny or various shades of brown, answering to the russet of the earth's surface . . .

How plain, wholesome, and earthy are the colors of quadrupeds generally! The commonest I should say is the tawny or various shades of brown, answering to the russet which is the prevailing color of the earth's surface, perhaps, and to the yellow of the sands beneath. The darker brown mingled with this answers to the darker-colored soil of the surface. The white of the polar bear, ermine weasel, etc., answers to the snow; the spots of the pards, perchance, to the earth spotted with flowers or tinted leaves of autumn; the black, perhaps, to night, and muddy bottoms and dark waters. There are few or no bluish animals.

Journal, February 21, 1855

Mule deer buck.

Love
Your Life

However mean your life is, meet it and live it; do not shun it and call it hard names. It is not so bad as you are. It looks poorest when you are richest. The fault-finder will find faults even in paradise. Love your life, poor as it is. You may perhaps have some pleasant, thrilling, glorious hours, even in a poorhouse. The setting sun is reflected from the windows of the almhouse as brightly as from the rich man's abode; the snow melts before its door as early in the spring.

The sand cherry adorned the sides of the path with its delicate flowers, which in the fall, weighed down with handsome cherries, fell over in wreaths like rays on every side . . .

My house was on the side of a hill, immediately on the edge of the larger wood, in the midst of a young forest of pitch pines and hickories, and half a dozen rods from the pond, to which a narrow footpath led down the hill. In my front yard grew the strawberry, blackberry, and life-everlasting, johnswort and goldenrod, shrub-oaks and sand cherry, blueberry and groundnut. Near the end of May, the sand cherry (*cerasus pumila*) adorned the sides of the path with its delicate flowers arranged in umbels cylindrically about its short stems, which last, in the fall, weighed down with good-sized and handsome cherries, fell over in wreaths like rays on every side.

Highbush cranberries.

New England meeting house.

There is nothing so fair, so pure as a lake;
sky water; it is a mirror no stone can crack . . .

ℏow peaceful the phenomena of the lake! Again the works of man shine as in the spring. Ay, every leaf and twig and stone and cobweb sparkles now at mid-afternoon as when covered with dew in a spring morning. Every motion of an oar or an insect produces a flash of light; and if an oar falls, how sweet the echo!

In such a day, in September or October, Walden is a perfect forest mirror, set round with stones as precious to my eye as if fewer or rarer. Nothing so fair, so pure, and at the same time so large, as a lake, perchance, lies on the surface of the earth. Sky water. It needs no fence. Nations come and go without defiling it. It is a mirror which no stone can crack, whose quicksilver will never wear off, whose gilding Nature continually repairs; no storms, no dust, can dim its surface ever fresh; a mirror in which all impurity presented to it sinks, swept and dusted by the sun's hazy brush—this the light dust-cloth—which retains no breath that is breathed on it, but sends its own to float as clouds high above its surface, and be reflected in its bosom still.

*Out of every crevice between the
dead leaves oozes some vehicle of color,
the unspent wealth of the year . . .*

We go admiring the pure and delicate tints of fungi on the surface of the damp swamp there, following up along the north side of the brook past the right of the old camp. There are many very beautiful lemon-yellow ones of various forms, some shaped like buttons, some becoming finely scalloped on the edge, some club-shaped and hollow, of the most delicate and rare but decided tints, contrasting well with the decaying leaves about them. There are others also pure white, others a wholesome red, others brown, and some even a light indigo-blue above and beneath and throughout. When colors come to be taught in the schools, as they should be, both the prism (or the rainbow) and these fungi should be used by way of illustration, and if the pupil does not learn colors, he may learn fungi, which perhaps is better. You almost envy the wood frogs and toads that hop amid such gems—some pure and bright enough for a breastpin. Out of every crevice between the dead leaves oozes some vehicle of color, the unspent wealth of the year, which Nature is now casting forth, as if it were only to empty herself.

Journal, September 1, 1856

Oyster mushroom.

Storm clouds over farm.

*I have surveyed the country on every
side within a dozen miles of where I live;
in imagination I have bought all the farms . . .*

At a certain season of our life we are accustomed to consider every spot as the possible site of a house. I have thus surveyed the country on every side within a dozen miles of where I live. In imagination I have bought all the farms in succession, for all were to be bought, and I knew their price. I walked over each farmer's premises, tasted his wild apples, discoursed on husbandry with him, took his farm at his price, at any price, mortgaging it to him in my mind; even put a higher price on it — took everything but a deed of it — took his word for his deed, for I dearly loved to talk — cultivated it, and him too to some extent, I trust, and withdrew when I had enjoyed it long enough, leaving him to carry it on.

I see young men, my townsmen, whose misfortune is to have inherited farms, houses, barns, cattle, and farming tools; for these are more easily acquired than got rid of. Better if they had been born in the open pasture and suckled by a wolf, that they might have seen with clearer eyes what field they were called to labor.

*Sometimes I sat in my sunny doorway rapt
in a revery amidst the pines and hickories . . .*

Sometimes, in a summer morning, having taken my accustomed bath, I sat in my sunny doorway from sunrise till noon, rapt in a revery, amidst the pines and hickories and sumachs, in undisturbed solitude and stillness, while the birds sang around or flitted noiseless through the house, until by the sun falling in at my west window, or the noise of some traveler's wagon on the distant highway, I was reminded of the lapse of time. I grew in those seasons like corn in the night, and they were far better than any work of the hands would have been.

For my panacea, instead of one of those quack vials of a mixture dipped from Acheron and the Dead Sea, which come out of those long shallow black-schooner-looking wagons which we sometimes see made to carry bottles, let me have a draught of undiluted morning air. Morning air! If men will not drink of this at the fountainhead of the day, why, then, we must even bottle up some and sell it in the shops, for the benefit of those who have lost their subscription ticket to morning time in this world. But remember, it will not keep quite till noonday even in the coolest cellar, but drive out the stopples long ere that and follow westward the steps of Aurora.

Sugar house.

Hearing a Different Drummer

Nature and human life are as various as our several constitutions. Who shall say what prospect life offers to another? Could a greater miracle take place than for us to look through each other's eyes for an instant? ...

If a man does not keep pace with his companions, perhaps it is because he hears a different drummer. Let him step to the music which he hears, however measured or far away.

Sometimes I rambled to pine groves, standing like temples, so soft and green and shady that the Druids would have worshipped in them . . .

Sometimes I rambled to pine groves, standing like temples, or like fleets at sea, full-rigged with wavy boughs, and rippling with light, so soft and green and shady that the Druids would have forsaken their oaks to worship in them; or to the cedar wood beyond Flints' Pond, where the trees, covered with hoary blue berries, spring higher and higher, are fit to stand before Valhalla, and the creeping juniper covers the ground with wreaths full of fruit; or to swamps where the usnea lichen hangs in festoons from the white-spruce trees, and toadstools, round tables of the swamp gods, cover the ground, and more beautiful fungi adorn the stumps, like butterflies or shells, vegetable winkles; where the swamp-pink and dogwood grow, the red alderberry glows like eyes of imps, the waxwork grooves and crushes the hardest woods in its folds, and the wild holly berries make the beholder forget his home with their beauty, and he is dazzled and tempted by nameless other wild forbidden fruits, too fair for mortal taste.

Vine maples and mossy Douglas fir trunks.

*How much beauty in decay! I pick up an
oak leaf, mingled red and green, October-like;
it is very beautiful held up to the light . . .*

How much beauty in decay! I pick up a white oak leaf,
dry and stiff, but yet mingled red and green, October-like,
whose pulpy part some insect has eaten beneath, exposing
the delicate network of its veins. It is very beautiful held up
to the light — such work as only an insect eye could
perform. Yet, perchance, to the vegetable kingdom such a
revelation of ribs is as repulsive as the skeleton in the
animal kingdom. In each case it is some little gourmand,
working for another end, that reveals the wonders of nature.
There are countless oak leaves in this condition now, and
also with a submarginal line of network exposed.

Journal, October 18, 1855

White oak leaves.

To him whose elastic and vigorous
thought keeps pace with the sun,
the day is a perpetual morning . . .

To him whose elastic and vigorous thought keeps pace with the sun, the day is a perpetual morning. It matters not what the clocks say or the attitudes and labor of men. Morning is when I am awake and there is a dawn in me.

Morning brings back the heroic ages. I was as much affected by the faint hum of a mosquito making its invisible and unimaginable tour through my apartment at earliest dawn, when I was sitting with door and windows open, as I could be by any trumpet that ever sang of fame.... The morning, which is the most memorable season of the day, is the awakening hour. Then there is at least somnolence in us; and for an hour, at least, some part of us awakes which slumbers all the rest of the day and night.

Black oak in morning mists.

*I paid many a visit to particular trees,
of kinds which are rare in this neighborhood,
standing in the middle of some pasture . . .*

Instead of calling on some scholar, I paid many a visit
to particular trees, of kinds which are rare in this neighborhood, standing far away in the middle of some pasture, or in
the depths of a wood or swamp, or on a hilltop; such as the
black birch, of which we have some handsome specimens
two feet in diameter; its cousin, the yellow birch, with its
loose golden vest, perfumed like the first; the beech, which
has so neat a bole and beautifully lichen-painted, perfect in
all its details, of which, excepting scattered specimens, I
know but one small grove of sizable trees left in the township, supposed by some to have been planted by the pigeons
that were once baited with beech nuts nearby.

Aspen grove.

*The innocence and beneficence of Nature,
such health, such cheer! Shall I not have
intelligence with the earth? Am I not partly
leaves and vegetable mould myself? . . .*

The indescribable innocence and beneficence of Nature—of sun and wind and rain, of summer and winter—such health, such cheer, they afford forever! and such sympathy have they ever with our race, that all Nature would be affected, and the sun's brightness fade, and the winds would sigh humanely, and the clouds rain tears, and the woods shed their leaves and put on mourning in mid-summer, if any man should ever for a just cause grieve. Shall I not have intelligence with the earth? Am I not partly leaves and vegetable mould myself?

Maple leaves and club mosses.

The stillness of the woods and the fields is remarkable at this season of the year. There is not even the creak of a cricket to be heard. Of myriads of dry shrub oak leaves, not one rustles. Your own breath can rustle them, yet the breath of heaven does not suffice to do so. The trees have the aspect of waiting for winter. The autumnal leaves have lost their color; they are now truly sere, dead, and the woods wear a somber color. Summer and harvest are over.

Journal, November 8, 1850

What is a country without rabbits and partridges? They are among the most simple and indigenous animal products; ancient and venerable families known to antiquity as to modern times; of the very hue and substance of Nature, nearest allied to leaves and to the ground — and to one another; it is either winged or it is legged. It is hardly as if you had seen a wild creature when a rabbit or a partidge bursts away, only a natural one, as much to be expected as rustling leaves. The partridge and the rabbit are still sure to thrive, like true natives of the soil, whatever revolutions occur.

*The stillness of the woods and fields
is remarkable at this season; the trees have
the aspect of waiting for winter . . .*

I seemed to remember the November evening
as a familiar thing come round again . . .

As the afternoons grow shorter, and the early evening drives us home to complete our chores, we are reminded of the shortness of life, and become more pensive at least in this twilight of the year. We are prompted to make haste and finish our work before the twilight comes. I leaned over a rail on the Walden road, waiting for the evening mail to be distributed, when such thoughts visited me. I seemed to remember the November evening as a familiar thing come round again, and yet I could hardly tell whether I had ever known it, or only divined it. It appeared like a part of a panorama at which I sat spectator, a part with which I was perfectly familiar, just coming into view. I foresaw how it would look and roll along and was prepared to be pleased. Just such a piece of art merely, infinitely sweet and good, did it appear to me, and just as little were any active duties required by me.... It was if I was promised the greatest novelty the world has ever seen or shall see, though the utmost possible novelty would be the difference between me and myself a year ago. This alone encouraged me, and was my fuel for the approaching winter. That we may behold the panorama with this slight improvement or change, this is what we sustain life for from year to year. And yet there is no more tempting novelty than this new November.

Journal. November 1, 1858

Waterfowl at dusk.

The Sun
Is a Morning Star

As I stand over the insect crawling amid
the pine needles on the forest floor, and
endeavoring to conceal itself from my sight, . . .
and hide its head from me who might, perhaps, be
its benefactor, and impart to its race some
cheering information, I am reminded of the greater
Benefactor and Intelligence that stand over me the
human insect . . . .

The light which puts out our eyes is darkness
to us. Only that day dawns to which we are
awake. There is more day to dawn. The sun is
but a morning star.

It struck me that these ghost leaves,
and the green ones whose form they assume,
were creatures of the same law . . .

Every tree, fence, and spire of grass that could raise its head above the snow was this morning covered with a dense hoar frost. The trees looked like airy creatures of darkness caught napping. On this side, they were huddled together, their gray hairs streaming, in a secluded valley, which the sun had not yet penetrated, and on that they went hurrying off in Indian file by hedgerows and watercourses, while the shrubs and grasses, like elves and fairies of the night, sought to hide their diminished heads in the snow. The branches and taller grasses were covered with a wonderful ice-foliage answering leaf for leaf to their summer dress. The center, diverging, and even more minute fibers, were perfectly distinct, and the edges regularly indented. These leaves were on the side of the twig or stubble opposite to the sun (when it was not bent toward the east), meeting it, for the most part, at right angles, and there were others standing out at all possible angles upon this, and upon one another.

It struck me that these ghost leaves, and the green ones whose form they assume, were creatures of the same law. It could not be in obedience to two several laws, that the vegetable juices swelled gradually into the perfect leaf on the one hand, and the crystalline particles trooped on their standard in the same admirable order on the other.

Journal, November 28, 1837

Frost on dead fern leaves.

Our first snow. The children greet it with a shout, when they come out at recess. It begins to whiten the plowed ground now, but has not overcome the russet of the grass ground. Birds generally wear the russet dress of nature at this season. They have their fall, no less than the plants. The bright tints depart from their foliage or feathers, and they flit past like withered leaves in rustling flocks. The sparrow is a withered leaf. Perchance I heard the last cricket of the season yesterday — they chirp here and there at longer and longer intervals till the snow quenches their song — and the last striped squirrel, too, perchance, yesterday. They then do not go into winter quarters till the ground is covered with snow.

Journal, November 8, 1853

*Live in each season as it passes; breathe
the air, drink the drink, taste the fruit,
and resign yourself to their influences . . .*

Live in each season as it passes; breathe the air, drink
the drink, taste the fruit, and resign yourself to the
influences of each. Let them be your only diet drink and
botanical medicines.

Journal, August 23, 1853

Why should we live with such hurry and waste of life?
We are determined to be starved before we are hungry. Men
say that a stitch in time saves nine, and so they take a
thousand stitches today to save nine tomorrow.

Frosted pumpkins.

Every leaf and twig was this morning covered with a sparkling ice armor, innumerable diamond pendants which jingled merrily . . .

Every leaf and twig was this morning covered with a sparkling ice armor; even the grasses in exposed fields were hung with innumerable diamond pendants, which jingled merrily when brushed by the foot of the traveler. It was literally the wreck of jewels and the crash of gems.

Journal, January 21, 1838

Walden, being like the rest usually bare of snow, or with only shallow and interrupted drifts on it, was my yard where I could walk freely when the snow was nearly two feet deep on a level elsewhere and the villagers were confined to their streets. There, far from the village street, and except at very long intervals, from the jingle of sleigh-bells, I slid and skated, as in a vast moose-yard well trodden, overhung by oak woods and solemn pines bent down with snow or bristling with icicles.

Icicles on willow branch.

Pines and spruces after a snowstorm.

*It is a surprising and memorable experience
to be lost in the woods during a snowstorm . . .*

It is a surprising and memorable, as well as valuable experience, to be lost in the woods anytime. Often in a snowstorm, even by day, one will come out upon a well-known road and yet find it impossible to tell which way leads to the village. Though he knows that he has traveled it a thousand times, he cannot recognize a feature in it, but it is as strange to him as if it were a road in Siberia. By night, of course, the perplexity is infinitely greater. In our most trivial walks, we are constantly, though unconsciously, steering like pilots by certain well-known beacons and headlands, and if we go beyond our usual course we will still carry in our minds the bearing of some neighboring cape; and not till we are completely lost, or turned around — for a man needs only to be turned round once with his eyes shut in this world to be lost — do we appreciate the vastness and strangeness of Nature. Every man has to learn the points of compass again as often as he awakes, whether from sleep or any abstraction. Not till we are lost, in other words, not till we have lost the world, do we begin to find ourselves, and realize where we are and the infinite extent of our relations.

Like the marmots in the hills, the pond closes its eyelids and becomes dormant for three months or more . . .

Every winter the liquid and trembling surface of the pond, which was so sensitive to every breath, and reflected every light and shadow, becomes solid to the depth of a foot or a foot and a half, so that it will support the heaviest teams, and perchance the snow covers it to an equal depth, and it is not to be distinguished from any level field. Like the marmots in the surrounding hills, it closes its eyelids and becomes dormant for three months or more. Standing on the snow-covered plain, as if in a pasture amid the hills, I cut my way first through a foot of snow, and then a foot of ice, and open a window under my feet, where, kneeling to drink, I look down into the quiet parlor of the fishes, pervaded by a softened light as through a window of ground glass, with its bright sanded floor the same as in summer; there a perennial waveless serenity reigns as in the amber twilight sky, corresponding to the cool and even temperament of the inhabitants. Heaven is under our feet as well as over our heads.

I also heard the whooping of the ice in the pond, my great bedfellow in that part of Concord, as if it were restless in its bed and would fain turn over, were troubled with flatulency and bad dreams; or I was waked by the cracking of the ground by the frost, as if some one had driven a team against my door, and in the morning would find a crack in the earth a quarter of a mile long and a third of an inch wide.

*After a still winter night I awoke
with the impression that some question had
been put to me; but there was dawning
Nature with no question on her lips . . .*

After a still winter night I awoke with the impression that some question had been put to me, which I had been endeavoring in vain to answer in my sleep, as what — how — when — where? But there was dawning Nature, in whom all creatures live, looking in my broad windows with serene and satisfied face, and no question on *her* lips. I awoke to an answered question, to Nature and daylight. The snow lying deep on the earth dotted with young pines, and the very slope of the hill on which my house is placed, seemed to say, Forward!

Snow-laden spruce tree.

All day long the squirrels came and went, and afforded me much entertainment . . .

In the course of the winter I threw out half a bushel of ears of sweet corn, which I had not got ripe, onto the snow crust by my door, and was amused by watching the motions of the various animals which were baited by it. In the twilight and the night the rabbits came regularly and made a hearty meal. All day long the red squirrels came and went, and afforded me much entertainment by their maneuvers.

At the approach of spring the red squirrels got under my house, two at a time, directly under my feet as I sat reading or writing, and kept up the queerest chuckling and chirruping and vocal pirouetting and gurgling sounds that ever were heard; and when I stamped they only chirruped the louder, as if past all fear and respect in their mad pranks, defying humanity to stop them. No you don't— chickaree—chickaree. They were wholly deaf to my arguments, or failed to perceive their force, and fell into a strain of invective that was irresistible.

Golden-mantled ground squirrel.

The Future Lies West

When I go out of the house for a walk, . . . I find, strange and whimsical as it may seem, that I finally and inevitably settle southwest, toward some particular wood or meadow or deserted pasture or hill in that direction. My needle is slow to settle, varies a few degrees, and does not always point due southwest, it is true, . . . but it always settles between west and south-southwest. The future lies that way to me, and the earth seems more unexhausted and richer on that side . . . . Eastward I go only by force; but westward I go free. . . . I believe that the forest which I see in the western horizon stretches uninterruptedly toward the setting sun, and there are no towns nor cities in it of enough consequence to disturb me. Let me live where I will, on this side is the city, on that the wilderness, ever I am leaving the city more and more, and withdrawing into and the wilderness. I should not lay so much stress on this fact, if I did not believe that something like this is the prevailing tendency of my countrymen.

"Walking"